Basic Procedures

for

Mobile Notary Signing Agents

by

Edward E. Peoples. DPA

Published

by

Meadow Crest Publishing on CreateSpace

Meadow Crest Publishing
P.O. Box 14885
Forestville, CA 95436
PH/FX: 707-887-1877

Preface

The purpose of this manual is to prepare notaries to perform the work of a loan signing agent. In most situations, the signing agent will deal with mortgage loan documents (docs) and will meet with borrowers to complete a loan closing. The docs will be for a re-finance (re-fi) of property, a purchase or sale of property, a reverse mortgage, an equity line of credit, or a loan modification. A section on auto document signing and government eVerify programs are included as well.

The content of the manual is practical, not theoretical, and based on current legal and ethical practices, and on my personal experiences and that of other signing agents. It provides a step-by-step guide to set up your signing agent business and to perform the job successfully right from the start. All the information can be applied immediately by the notary, with only minor variations dictated by the various notary laws within the several states.

Table of Contents

Chapter 1 - The Role of a Mobile Notary Signing Agent

The Notary Signing Agent

A mobile notary signing agent is a state licensed or commissioned notary public who works as an independent contractor to witness the signings of loan documents by borrowers. Certain documents in a loan document package, such as a deed of trust, mortgage, certificate of trust, or signature affidavit require notarization, either with an acknowledgement or a *jurat*, whereas many of the related documents just require the borrower's signature or initials.

The signing requirements often vary between lenders and/or title companies. Some want blue ink, some want black ink. Some want a copy of the borrower's identity documents, some don't. Signing company requirements often vary as well. Sometimes a notary is required to fax back certain documents to the signing company before dropping off the documents package with a courier. Sometimes not. Only experience and a careful reading of the notary instructions that come with the signing order and with documents will provide the notary the required direction.

Typically, the loans encumber real estate for security, and the notary will be working with real estate loan documents. However, automotive document signing is a growing category of loan signing for notaries, as an increasing number of individuals purchase cars on-line; and the signing/closing is completed by a notary.

There also is a growing need to maintain data security within the bio-pharmaceutical, medical research fields, and the aerospace and defense industries, has created a relatively new category of signing in which the notary verifies the identity of the individual who is then allowed access to specific computer data within his or her company or research field. These special categories of loan document signing are detailed in Chapter 7. The first six chapters focus exclusively on the notary signing agent's role in real estate loan documents signing.

The Loan Process

The loan process involves several players, and usually begins by a borrower applying for a loan through a loan broker, either in person or on-line. That broker refers the loan to a lender that offers the interestand conditions best suited to the borrower's wants, and for which the borrower qualifies. After the loan is approved, the matter is then referred to a title company to prepare the documents.

These documents invariable include a note and mortgage or deed of trust by which the borrower puts up his or her real estate property as security for a loan. An array of additional documents is included, depending upon the type of loan and the lender requirements. Typical transactions involve a loan to purchase or sell a residence or commercial property, to re-finance existing property, to obtain a line of credit, or (for seniors over age 62) to obtain a reverse mortgage. Specific examples of the different types of loans and their accompanying documents are discussed in a later chapter.

The Signing

The title company usually refers the documents to a signing company, a firm that in essence acts as a broker of document signings, who in turn refers the documents to a notary signing agent living and/or working near to where the borrower lives and/or where the signing will take place. The documents are either sent as attachments on e-mails or are sent buy an overnight courier. On rare occasion, they are sent to the borrower. The actual signing might take place in a residence, an office, a motel room, a café, a park, or a car; wherever it is convenient for the borrowers. Be prepared.

Often a borrower has talked with the loan broker on the phone, but never in person, and the notary is the only live person the borrower meets during the entire process. Consequently, it is crucial that the notary present the best professional image. He or she not only represents the notary profession, but the title company and lender as well. In a way it is like the closing of any transaction, the borrower/client should come away feeling satisfied, with no regrets and no unanswered questions.

This is particularly important when signing a reverse mortgage. The notary signing agent meets with the borrowers to guide them through the signing process and to witness their signatures and to legally verify their identities and their their willingness and competence to sign the documents. It is important that all documents be signed or initialed where required and that each notarization is complete, or you, the notary might be called upon   to return to complete the signing at you own expense. Also, as a consequence, you might not hear from that signing company again. The signature of borrower must be exactly as it appear on the documents, and when initialing, the borrower needs to use all initials contained in the signature/s.

Variations in Notary Duties Between States

States vary as to what role they allow a notary to have, so as a notary, be familiar with the specifics of the state laws in which you intend to work. Also you need to know in advance of any restrictions or requirements necessary for recording documents in one state that you notarize in your own state. For example, Florida, Connecticut, and South Carolina require two witnesses to a signing, and one may be a notary. Some states require an attorney be present or involved in the signing. What does your state require? If you are notarizing documents for a property located in another state and the documents will be filed in that other state, and that other state requires an attorney to be present at the signing, the title company will provide you with the name and phone number of the attorney that they have hired, and you will conduct the signing and notarization with the borrower and with the attorney on the phone to provide any directions necessary and to comply with the law.

States might also vary as to the evidence a notary must have to legalize the notarization process. For example, prior to 2008 in a California acknowledgment, the wording called for a notary to have **either** personal knowledge of the signer or satisfactory evidence as to his or her identity. The notary would line out which type of evidence that did not apply.

As of January 2, 2008, the wording changed and California notaries cannot use *personal knowledge* as a basis of identity (an exception is described in a later chapter). New acknowledgment forms were required that did not contain the words *personal knowledge*. However, it took months for knowledge of this change in the required wording to reach all the title companies and lenders. In the meantime, a notary had to draw a line through the lender's entire acknowledgment and attach one with the appropriate legal wording. This might still be the case.

Check with your state's notary regulations to determine what wording you may use on an acknowledgment or a jurat if the document will be filed in a state other than your own. For example, in

California, I may use an acknowledgment provided on an out-of-state document provided that I am acknowledging the appearance and signing before me, I only acknowledge the identity of the signer and not any position he or she might hold, and the wording *personally known to me* is not included on the form. On the other hand, I must use the exact wording on a jurat as stated in the state's notary manual, no matter where the document will be filed. Consequently, I frequently find the need to attach my own jurat to a document and I then place a stamp over the unacceptable worded jurat that says *see attached.*

What Notaries Are Not

As a general rule, notaries are not lawyers, loan brokers , or CPAs. Therefore, a notary **may not** offer legal or financial advice. Also, the notary does not work for the borrower. As an independent contractor, a notary works at the moment for whomever contracted for the signing and pays for the job: usually the signing company, but occasionally a title company or bank. The notary **may not** offer opinions nor give any advice about any aspect of the loan. He or she is a facilitator of the signing process and a witness to the identification of the signers. As such, he or she may explain what is included in a document or where to find specific items, but he or she **may not, must not,** make judgments as to the worth of the loan.

If a borrower has a question about any aspect of the loan or documents, have him or her immediately phone the loan broker who initiated the process with the borrower. Often the broker has given the borrower his or her phone number and has told the borrower to call regarding any question. The notary will also have the phone number of the broker or title company escrow representative handling the loan.

If you, as a notary, have any questions about signing requirements, call your signing company or the title company escrow officer; don't guess or leave the signing in doubt.

Any time the documents show that the property is held in a trust, usually a family trust, **always** ask your contact person from the signing company or title company how the borrowers should sign. Some want the borrowers to actually write the word "Trustee" after their signature on any documents that have that form typed below the signature line, and some do not want the word "Trustee" to be written out. Never assume that the same rules apply with all signings. It all depends on who the lender is and who the title company is. Always clarify the signing procedures each time the occasion arises with a trust.

Chapter 2: Establishing Your Mobile Notary Business Profile

Secure Your Notary Commission

I stated in the *Preface* that the information presented herein assumes that the reader has his or her notary license or commission, has some familiarity with notarizing, and is ready to take on the role of a role signing agent, either full or part time. By the term *secure*, I mean make sure that you have a current and clean copy of your certificate or license, and notary bond, because you will need it later to fax copies to the signing companies for whom you want to work.

Choosing a Certification Course

As a notary, you are duly authorized to notarize any legal documents, as stipulated by the law of the state in which you work. You really do not need to meet any additional standards or qualifications to legally work as a loan signing agent. Nevertheless, you need to complete a signing agent course and be certified by a recognized organization or association if you expect to obtain work by companies. Certification is equated with capability and professionalism in the minds of prospective employers.

There are many companies that offer training and certification, but some of them offer courses merely as a source of their income, and not to set a standard for you are accepted by the field. There are also many that provide good quality training and certification, such as the Academy for Notaries, or Notary Rotary, but their certification might not give you full nation-wide acceptance. There is one company that provides it all: training, certification, and background screening: the National Notary Association (NNA).

The NNA is recognized throughout the notary, signing company, and title company industry as the standard everyone seeks to meet. Lenders and title companies want their document signing and notarizing to be performed by a reliable, trained, and trustworthy notary. When you are applying to a signing company to be considered as an independent notary contractor, mobile signing agent, a faxed copy of a certificate that says *NNA certified and Background Screened Notary Signing Agent* meets the qualifications of many lenders.

I do not work for NNA, nor do I have any financial interest in the company, but I look to them for many of my notary needs: training, certification, notary supplies, a notary bond, and E & O insurance. Specialized training and education opportunities are also available (discussed in Chapter 7). The company is also politically active in the best interests of notaries, and works with various levels of government to establish the latest in notary procedures. As a member of NNA, one has ready access to legal advice about any specific question about signing documents. They are only a phone call away. Check out their web site and you will see what I mean.

Supplemental Training and Certification

You can complete the NNA certification course and take the exam on-line. You will become certified when you pass their exam, and you will learn valuable information during the process. However, there is no substitute for in-class, face-to-face instruction. Check you your local community colleges for their regular or community education offerings. Courses could include real estate procedures, real estate finance, escrow, and notary training. Never stop learning.

After completing the NNA course and receiving certification, I took a another course in becoming a mobile notary signing agent through my local community offered by a private company, the Academy for Notaries. I learned a great deal in the class room setting by dealing with the actual documents involved in signing, and I learned a great deal of practical knowledge from the experienced notary signing agent who taught the course. She has also been available as a resource for additional information, special notary forms, and clarification of notary questions and issues.

Choosing a Business Name

Choose a name that is relatively short, concise, and memorable. Write down as many different names as come to mind, wait several days, and then review the list. You want a name that will work on business cards, as an e-mail address, and as a web site title. When you think you have the perfect choice, go to a web name search site, such as *Go Daddy*, and enter you chosen name to search its availability. It might already be taken. Enter several names and see which ones stand out, and don't be in a hurry to settle on one name. You will be using it in many ways and, hopefully, for a long time.

Choosing How to Conduct Business

There are three primary ways one can conduct a business: (1) as an individual, (2) a corporation, or (3) partnership. I am assuming that partnership is not a consideration in most cases. That leaves as an individual or a corporation. You can form a corporation, thereby possibly limiting your personal liability. It is easy to complete the incorporation process yourself for less than $200. Check the web site of Nolo Press. You will find their book on how to do it, and it contains all the directions and forms to quickly and easily incorporate.

If you choose what is termed an "S" corporation, profits are automatically passed on to you as an individual and there is no corporate tax. On the other hand, your state might have a corporate tax. For example, in California, the State Franchise Tax Board taxes the corporation at a percentage of the income or $800.00, whichever is greater, with an exemption for the first year. So you are out $800.00 at the least. Also, it is very questionable that you can minimize your personal liability since you are commissioned or appointed a notary as an individual.

It hardly seems worth the effort of incorporating unless you plan to eventually establish your own signing company, which will be difficult at best. My suggestion is to go to the county clerk and file a *doing business as* (DBA) form, then follow the clerk's directions in publishing it in a local paper. Now you are (fictitious) James J. Meeker, DBA as *Meeker's Mobile Notary*.

The single most important advantage this gives you is that you can obtain a tax identification number (TIN) from the IRS (go on their web site and apply on-line), and then you do not have to use your social security number in any communication. So when the singing company you have applied to for work asks that your personal information be sent to them by fax, you use your TIN; unless you like having your social security number sent out hither and yon via fax. Thereby, you are minimizing identity theft. Also, you are telling the singing companies that you are not just John or Mary Clod, you are DBA a company.

Your Business Card

Your business card should contain your business name, your name, the title *Mobile Notary Signing Agent*, your business e-mail address, your web site address, if youhave one, your cell phone number, and one land line phone number. Keep the design simple and professional looking. Now all this having been said, you need to know that you won't be handing out your card very often during loan signings.

You will be prohibited from soliciting any notary business from a borrower while you are working with him, her, or them on documents for a signing company. However, if a borrower asks you for a card, explain that you "are not there to solicit business, but if at some future time he or she needs a notary, please feel free to call me," then give him or her your card.

As a way of getting started in business, I suggest that you distribute your business cards to hospitals, life care facilities, residential centers, jails, and prisons. Keep in mind, however, that current valid identification might not be readily available to individuals at these locations, so if called to such a location, always verify that such I.D. is available before traveling there.

Make it a point to personally contact and give a card to the appropriate individuals at banks, savings and loans, credit unions, and title companies who play a role in selective notaries for work. There was a time when all these institutions had their own notaries on the payroll. However, many now find the record keeping a hassle and the liability exposure to great to maintain a paid notary. Keep in mind in all this that these local institutions will not be the primary source for you signing work. That will come from the signing companies. However, they might offer selected signings that you can cite as experience when applying to a signing company.

Basic Procedures for Mobile Notary Signing Agents

Your Computer and Printer Capabilities

Your primary source of business will come from signing companies via e-mails with documents attached. There might be several attachments on any given e-mail. As with your business card, keep you e-mail address concise and memorable, and separate from your personal e-mail address.

Your computer connection should be either DSL or cable, not dial-up. You want your contacts to be fast, reliable, and capable of handling large numbers of pages in a document. The typical document package will be run between 90 to 130 pages, but up to 200 pages are possible. That means your e-mail account needs to be able to accept a lot of megabytes.

Your computer and printer will comprise your basic work equipment. You should keep your software current. **You must have a laser printer**, with the capability of printing both letter and legal size documents. **If you don't have a laser printer, you won't get any work at all.** A two-tray laser printer, with fax capability, is the ideal. But you can switch back and forth between sizes if your printer only has one tray. You also need to have the capability of faxing and receiving both letter and legal size documents.

Web Site Availability

Many notary signing agents have web sites, but it is not really necessary. If you are considering having a web site, go on-line and search the web for notaries.

You will see an array of styles and content presentations to use as examples. If you have taken my advice given above about selecting a business name, you already know if your name is available as a web site. Personally, I like the extra exposure that a web site offers and enjoy creating and modifying my on site. It is also ego satisfying. It has been the source of some business as well.

You don't need to have any particular expertise to create your own web site. Companies such as *Go Daddy* or *1on1.com* will take you through all the steps and host it for you. Your e-mail service provider might offer the same service.

If you have the time and inclination, establish a web site name and reserve it through one of the many web companies. I use *Go Daddy* only as an example and because they are easy to use. You can create your own site using the many sources available on line.

I am technologically challenged, but I created a very useful one-page web site using a program called *Dreamweaver*. If you are so inclined, buy the condensed version of their book entitled *Creating a Web Page in Dreamweaver*, by Nolan Hester, published by Peachpit Press in Berkeley, CA, available at your local book stores. The more complete Dreamweaver manual is too complex for my challenged mind to comprehend.

Insuring Yourself in the Workplace

Working as a notary places you in a position of responsibility and corresponding liability. If a loan goes south because of your errors or negligence, you could be liable in court for money damages. Most of you reading this probably will never need protection, but just in case, buy some coverage.

In most states you are required to post a bond with the county clerk, in an amount from $10,000 to $15,000, depending upon your state, but that still leaves you exposed for liability. Errors and Omissions insurance is not necessary to work as a notary, but it is strongly suggested that you obtain E & O coverage of at least $25,000. $100,000 is recommended and is available at an affordable cost through NNA and elsewhere. Most signing companies for whom you will work require that amount. Think of the cost as two signings for the year, and you can rest easy.

Creating a Document Library

On your computer create a new folder titled *Common Notary forms*. Make copies of all the notary forms you might use, wording them as required in your state. These could include the following: acknowledgment, *jurat*, subscribing witness statement, power of attorney copy, signing by a X, signature/AKA affidavit, compliance agreement, and corrections agreement, to name but a few.

Most states have specific wording requirements

for the two primary forms: the acknowledgment and

jurat. Note that additional information has been inserted in the lower portion of the acknowledgment and *jurat* you will find on some forms that you can purchase from notary supply companies.   This extra information is not necessary, but it will be very useful if you need to attach one to a document. You can identify the documents so there will not be any confusion about what it represents.

The Hold Harmless Agreement
You might often find a document called a *hold harmless agreement* included as an attachment to an e-mail signing order from the signing company that hires you. It is intended to limit the liability of the signing company. You have the borrower/s sign it and fax it back to the signing company or keep in a file for them. I have found it useful to present my own *Assignment Disclosure and Hold Harmless Agreement*   to the borrowers for signing.

My own agreement shown at the back of this manual goes beyond what one usually finds in those by signing companies, with a new title, and includes an explanation of my role as a notary and the admonishment wording that notaries must give to a signers about swearing or affirming that they are stating the truth, etc. I have the borrower affirm the admonishment. When I complete a signing, I staple it to the back of the signing instructions as a part of that signing file.

I can't give legal advice, but I believe the borrower's signature/s on this agreement offers sufficient proof that they knew my role, and knew the oath I gave them when notarizing their signature/s. Please feel free to copy and/or modify this form to suit your needs.

The Mobile Notary Assignment Summary

If you want to do well in business, you need to be organized from the start. As a part of that effort, I suggest using a one-page assignment summary that contains all the information relevant to your signing: information about the borrower/s; the signing referral; signing status (completed, cancelled, refused to sign), completed document delivery; and a description of the documents you notarized. Check the Appendix for a sample you may use.

The signing company usual will want you to phone or fax in a report soon after you have completed a signing. They usually will want the Signing #, name of the borrower, name of the courier company you used to return the documents, and the tracking number. If you take a moment now to review the *Mobile Notary Assignment Summary* in the Appendix, you will note that all this is there. I staple this to the signing order e-mail, signing instructions, hold harmless agreement, and tracking results form, and keep it in an organized file.

Some of the signing companies will have you update the signing status on their web site. For that you will be given a user name and password when you contract with the company so that you can login and complete an update.

Notary Accessories

You will need a small case, sufficient to hold your notary journal, a few files containing extra forms, and a small bag containing your notary stamp or seal, and a few additional items. It also must be capable of being locked, for the security of your notary stamp. Check with notary supply companies, such as Notary Rotary, Academy for Notaries, or NNA for their products. You will also need a finger ink pad, because the notarization of certain documents requires a fingerprint placed in your journal, along with the signature. I also suggest you buy an ink pad and several rubber name stamps for your name, state, county, phone number, and the words *notary public*.

Chapter 3: National Signing Companies:
Your Source of Work

Choosing and Soliciting Signing Companies

I explained in Chapter 1 that a signing company is, in essence, a broker for document signing. One signing company might process all the loan document signings for a number of titles companies located throughout the country. The signing company contracts with a number of notaries and selects an available notary who works near to where the borrowers live. You want to be that notary in your area. You want them to call you first.

Ideally, you want a signing company that does substantial business in your area and pays well or at least pays promptly. Like a lot of ideals, this one is not easy to find. Some of them are slow pay, as much as two months after a signing. However, there is one source that is helpful in determining which signing companies to solicit: **www.notaryrotary.com**.

Notary Rotary is a company that provides an array of services and products for notaries. They offer training courses, certificates, and most any type of product a notary might want. They also serve as a notary locator for someone seeking a notary in any given area in the nation. Membership in Notary Rotary is available at two levels: basic (free) and Premier (paid), and membership offers access to their services.

It is well worth it.

We are concerned now with a special service provided by Notary Rotary, signing company listings. On their website, at the top, you will see six blue colored tabs with names. Select the fourth tab over from the left, labeled "Signing Service Listings." When you open that sub-site, you will find most of the national signing companies listed, from A to Z, and each one is rated by a process that includes input from notaries who have dealt with them. Each listing is hypertexed, meaning that you can open up each one and read comments from other notaries: who pays and who doesn't. For example, click on a low rated company, then click on comments, and you will understand the value of knowing this information before you take a signing. You can also note the states in which a signing company does most of its business by the notary comments.

This service by Notary Rotary can be invaluable. I learned the hard way. A signing company that I had not solicited called me to complete two signings, one single document signing for $50. and one home refinance loan (re-fi) loan for $75.00. They had located me from the NNA certificated notary site. I accepted and completed the signings. After two months has elapsed without receiving payment, I contact them and got that age-old response, "the check is in the mail," or "your name is in the queue and should be sent out any day now." After another three months passed, I started looking for sources to help me collect. I did not find any.

I did learn that the signing company, a corporation, was not accountable to any one or any government agency for their conduct, and the only recourse I had was to sue the company. It was then that I looked the company up on Notary Rotary and read comments from many notaries that had not been paid by them as well. Had I read these comments before, I would have declined the signing assignments.

I stumbled upon some inside information about the signing company, by mere chance, and used it to again request payment. They paid me within the week. I was lucky, and I have been careful ever since about which companies I choose. Also be cautious about signing up with so-called signing services that charge you to be listed. They aren't going to hire you.

Signing Company Requirements

By using this Notary Rotary signing list, you can access the web site of each company and you will see how to apply for consideration to work for them as a mobile notary signing agent. Some on the companies will respond immediately, some at a later time, and some will not respond.

When a signing company accepts your request to sign up with them for signing assignments, they will send you an e-mail with an attachment and require you to sign an Independent Contractor Agreement and fax in a W-9 tax form (note the DBA - tax I.D. number). They probably will also ask that you fax a copy of your notary commission, and your NNA screened and certified certificate, your bond and your E & O insurance policy.

Occasionally you will find a signing company that will not accept applications from a notary until that person has worked for a year or even two years, or has completed 100 or 200 signings. Don't be discouraged. Your opportunities for acceptance will increase with your experience.

You might also find a company that requires you to take and successfully pass an exam on information related to loan documents, their policies, and their requirements for notaries to follow during signings. Be familiar with the basic loan documents reviewed in subsequent chapters: what is their purpose and what information do they contain. For example, what is contained in the Truth in Lending, Good Faith Estimate, and HUD Settlement Statements?

Signing Company Payment Policies

You will find over time that each signing company has its own payment policy which is usually stated in their contractor's agreement. Some want an invoice from you at the end of a month, and they pay by the end of the following month. Others require you tolog into their web site and report each signing when it is completed. This confirms the completed signing and serves as you invoice as well. Some use direct deposit and pay regularly.

Make a list of these requirements so that you can be current on the requirements of each, and file invoices to those requiring them. One thing is for certain, some signing companies are slow pay. I suggest that you track your signings and payments in an organized fashion.

Creating a Business Spread Sheet

One of the best ways to track signing, and payments for them, is to develop a signing spread sheet. Create titles for orders from signing companies such as: date received, borrower name, signing company and order number, town, purpose, fee, mileage travelled, date completed, date billed, date received payment. This will also serve you well when preparing for tax time. Your taxable income and miles travelled are readily available.

You might even include a space in that spread sheet for listing the number of documents notarized during each signing. The reason for this is to compare the total amount paid for a signing with how much each signature notarized would be worth if you were paid per notarization. You will report your total earnings to the IRS and to your state tax agency each year, but oddly enough, it is my understanding that money earned by a notary, on a per-signature notarization basis is exempt from reporting to Social Security as self-employment income, unless one wants to report it to earn retirement benefits. I don't mean any of this as tax advice, so check with your tax preparer or the IRS for confirmation.

If you are a relatively young person and want to establish work quarters to eventually qualify for social security payments, you would want to report all you self-employed notary income. However, if you are retired, or have sufficient income for retirement from other sources, I understand that you can choose to exempt your notary income from self-employment tax..

The fee one may charge for notarizing a signature on a document is set by the Secretary of State, but the fee you receive from a signing company is for the signing, not for each signature notarized. For example, the fee a notary may charge for a signature on an acknowledgment or *jurat* in California is $10. Suppose I complete twenty signings for which I am paid $100. each and notarize the borrower's signature on four documents at each signing ($40. worth). My total income for those signings is $2,000, but $800. is exempt from self-employment tax (20 signings x $40.) Again, check with your tax preparer or the IRS for the details.

Establishing Your Signing Fees

For the most part, signing companies set the fees by what they will offer you for a given signing. However, fees do vary from company to company. Market conditions also have an influence. The nature of the signing will also affect the fee. Most signings are either for re-fis, new purchases, or equity lines of credit. In today's market the going rate seems to be about $50. To $75. if the documents are sent by courier (Fed Ex or UPS, etc.) and $75. To $100. for e-mail documents. The extra $25. allegedly is to pay your time and expense to print out two sets of documents. Companies seem to pay more for reverse mortgage signings. For me, that has varied between $80. to $100. I expect these fees to increase when the housing market improves and business is better for everyone.

There are times, however, when a company will call you to request a signing and ask you how much you would charge. It will pay you to know the travel distances within the county or area in which you work to help you in determining the worth of a signing to you. I also take into consideration the hour of the day or night for the signing and the time of year. I might charge more to travel twenty-five mile to the coast on a narrow winding road at night in the winter than I would in the center of town at noon in June. Don't underestimate your worth.

The typical signing for me involves two borrowers, a man and wife, so I print one set of documents for them. However, if there are multiple borrowers, say two couples buying an investment property and each couple wants a set of the documents, I would charge an additional fee of $20. to $25.

Experience will guide you in setting your fees, or in working for those signings companies that pay more and pay sooner. You will find that some loans, and some lenders and/or title companies require more work than others. For example, one lender might require that the borrower initial every page that is not signed, whereas another lender does not require the initializing. As another consideration, if a signing company calls you at the last minute for a signing that afternoon, or in an hour, it might be that their regular notary was busy, and they need to find another notary at the last minute. That type of situation might warrant you asking for an additional $10. or $15.00.

Chapter 4: Types of Loans and Loan Documents

Primary Disclosures: The Basic Loan Document Series

The presentation and signing of the loan documents creates the structure of the real estate loan. They establish the following:

➢ loan amount, cost of the loan, and repayment provision

➢ security for the loan, and the obligation by the borrower

➢ the identity of the borrower/s

➢ disclosures by the lender to the borrower

➢ disclosures by the borrower to the lender

This structure of the loan is built within the framework of real estate mortgage laws. There are certain documents common to all loans, primarily because of the requirements of these laws. As a notary signing agent, you will familiar with these required documents and with the documents that, though not required, are often included with a document package for the signing. Before examining the particular documents, we will first review what I consider to be at the heart of mortgage lending law, RESPA.

The Real Estate Settlement Procedures Act (RESPA)

RESPA is a consumer protection statute, first passed in 1974, for the purposes: (1) helping consumers become better shoppers for settlement services; and (2), eliminating kickbacks and referral fees that unnecessarily increase the costs of certain settlement services.

RESPA requires that borrowers receive disclosures at various times. Some disclosures spell out the costs associated with the settlement, outline lender servicing and escrow account practices and describe business relationships between settlement service providers. RESPA also prohibits certain practices that increase the cost of settlement services.

Section 8 of RESPA prohibits a person from giving or accepting any- thing of value for referrals of settlement service business related to a federally related mortgage loan. It also prohibits a person from giving or accepting any part of a charge for services that are not performed.

Section 9 of RESPA prohibits home sellers from requiring home buyers to purchase title insurance from a particular company.

RESPA covers loans secured with a mortgage placed on a one-to-four family residential property. These include most purchase loans, assumptions, refinances, property improvement loans, and equity lines of credit. These also include the types of loans that will be the subjects of your signing work.

When borrowers apply for a mortgage loan, mortgage brokers and/or lenders must give the borrowers certain specific bits of information, or disclosures, as follows:

> ➢ a **Good Faith Estimate** (GFE) of settlement costs, which lists the charges the buyer is likely to pay at settlement. This is only an estimate and the actual charges may differ. If a lender requires the borrower to use a particular settlement provider, then the lender must disclose this requirement on the GFE.

> ➢ a **Mortgage Servicing Disclosure Statement**, which discloses to the borrower whether the lender intends to service the loan or transfer it to another lender. It also provides information about complaint resolution.

> ➢ **Affiliated business arrangement statement** in which the lender must inform the borrower that he or she may use any other provider of services and is not required to use those that are owned by or controlled by the lender or common corporate parent.

> ➢ The **HUD-1 Settlement Statement**, discussed below.

➢ The **escrow account operation and disclosures Statement**, in which shows all the expected deposits and disbursements into and from an impound account

This is what it required under RESPA. The purpose of providing the borrower with a GFE is to let him or her know the cost of the loan process with a particular borrower, or through a particular loan broker, so that the borrower can shop around for the best loan. From my experience, this rarely happens. Borrowers either don't know they can shop or they choose not to shop, and they feel committed to the loan as presented.

Don't ask the borrower when you are preparing to complete the singing if he or she has been provided with this RESPA information. You will find that the information is contained within the documents package you brought to the signing. The borrower will have been given a copy of the GFE, probably by his or her loan broker, but he or she might not have reviewed it thoroughly until you are there at the signing/closing of the loan. It actually seems irrelevant to the loan once the HUD Settlement Statement is provided.

You may show the borrower where certain cost item are found, but **NEVER** comment on the appropriateness of the costs or fees contained therein. These are just estimates, anyway, and the borrower should have already discussed the costs with his or her loan broker. If the borrower has any more questions, have him or her phone the loan broker right then.

The HUD -1 Settlement Statement

The Settlement Statement is a standard form that clearly shows all charges and fees paid by the borrower. He or she will probably look these figures over carefully, and perhaps compare them with those on the GFE. RESPA allows the borrower to request to see this HUD-1 Settlement Statement one day before the actual settlement and closing. However, don't ask the borrower if he or she has seen the statement because you have a copy in the loan document package for them to sign, and chances are that they did not know they could see it earlier.

Before you go to a signing location, check the bottom line on page 1 of the HUD to see if the borrower/s are to provide funds for the loan to close. If funds are due, I always call the borrower to ascertain if he or she is aware of it and if they will have a personal or bank check for me at the time of the signing.

This is one of the most important documents to have the borrower sign, where indicated and, often initial pages as well. A sample copy of the HUD-1 for is in the Appendix for your review.

Truth in Lending Statement

The Consumer Credit Protection Act, commonly known as the Truth-in-Lending Act, became effective in May 1968. This is a disclosure statement designed to show a borrower several specifics about the loan: the amount financed by the loan; the interest rate; the annual percentage rate (APR); the amount of the payment, including interest and principal; and the total amount of money paid over the life of the loan if it is taken to maturity.

The APR will differ and often be slightly higher than the interest rate cited and that might be questioned by the borrower. The APR is the rate that results when the amount of the loan is combined into a single figure that also includes all the fees and charges, such as the borrower's prepaid discount points, loan fees, loan finder fees, loan service fees, loan broker fees, etc.

Secondary Disclosures

There are a number of other types of disclosures you will find in a loan document package that cover the following: appraisal, balloon payment, credit and fair lending, earthquake and other hazards, mortgage loan application, and prepayment penalty, to name but a few. Some of these disclosures must be signed and some initialed by the borrower, as indicated on the disclosure forms.

The borrower must also provide disclosures about his or her identity and its variations, signature, marital or domestic partnership status, residential history, and employment history.   In most loan situations, the borrower must also agree to cooperate with the lender in making any necessary corrections to the documents, such as spelling or typo errors, but not to the essence of the loan itself.   A doc called a Corrections Agreement is included with most document packages and might or might not require notariaetion.

Documents Requiring Notarization

Of the 80 to 150 pages of documents you as notary might take to the signing, on average only three to six documents will actually require notarization. These might include either a Mortgage or Deed of Trust (regular loan or reverse mortgage), Signature or AKA Affidavit, Corrections Agreement, Certificate of Trust, Occupancy and Financial Status Affidavit, and Compliance Agreement. Some variations of these documents are found in most types of loans. In certain situations a Grant Deed and a quitclaim deed might also be used.

Disclosures to Sign

There might be an occasional odd document that requires notarization, so examine the loan package completely. Most of the other pages are filled with a variety Riders and disclosures that require the borrower's signature.

The following are some of the disclosures that require the borrower's signature to acknowledge the receipt of the documents: Credit Scores; for Voluntary Escrow Account; Good Faith Estimate; Truth in Lending; Private Mortgage Insurance; Impound Account; Right to Appraisal Report; Interim Interest Payment; Domestic Partnership Addendum to Uniform residential Loan Application; Occupancy Affidavit and financial Status; Insurance; and RESPA Servicing; along with IRS forms 4506-T and W-9.

As a second caution, be sure to review all the documents to determine which require signatures, initials, or completion.

Chapter 5: How to Prepare and Complete
the Actual Document Signing

The Signing Referral

One day your phone will ring and when you answer, someone will say, "This is John Doe of Triple X Signing Services. Can you handle a signing for us?" Your first signing!! WOW !! Now you know that you have arrived, but there are several questions you need to ask before accepting the signing:

➢   When is the signing? Often they will want it today and think that your work world revolves around their requirements. Seriously, it will probably be in a day or so.

➢   What type of signing is it? A regular re-fi, new purchase, line of credit, etc. with one or two borrowers is standard, but if it becomes more complex, you need to charge accordingly.

➢   Where is the signing? Know the area you serve and the mileage from location to location, and where you will or will not go.

➢   How much do you pay for this?   Fees vary to some degree, but as mentioned earlier, e-mail docs of a regular signing pay between $70. to $100, and overnight docs from $50. to $60. Request more if the elements of the signing warrant it.

➢ When will the e-mail docs arrive? The docs usually are sent from the title company and might not arrive until a few hours before the scheduled signing. Press for plenty of time.

➢ Are the documents attachments to the e-mail letter or legal seize, or mixed or separated? Usually, the HUD Settlement Statement is legal size and others are mixed. Hopefully the sender has sorted them according to size when attaching them to the e-mail. If you have a two tray printer, no problem.

➢ Ask, where did you obtain my name to call me? Often, with a new signing company, they got your name and information off of national site such as NNA, Notary Café, Notary Rotary, Need a Notary, or other sites. If you know where your referrals come from it will help you decide where to spend money in continuing a sign-up listing.

Note that when I accept a signing, there are certain locations in my county that would require me to drive a narrow and winding road along steep cliffs, which I can't do. I tell the signing company that I can't drive there, but I can meet the borrower somewhere convenient to both of us. It has always worked, and we have met at coffee shops, restaurants, parks, and businesses.

Preparing to Receive the Signing Docs

Within minutes of accepting a signing, you will receive an e-mail confirming the signing and containing signing instructions. It will probably show a time for the signing and ask you to confirm that time with the borrower. Make the call, confirm the time, and then report the confirmation to the signing company. Always keep them informed of the signing process. It lessens their anxiety.

When you initially talk with the borrower, confirm the address for the signing and get any specific directions necessary to locate it. Advise the borrower that you will need to see a valid current identification for all those who sign, usually a driver's license. I ask the borrower to make a copy of the driver's licenses to enclose with the returned docs. This is sometimes required to satisfy Homeland Security as to the borrower's identity. A passport or other ID accepted in your state will suffice. Note, that a foreign passport usually is acceptable ID **only** if it has been stamped by the US government immigration officials.

It might save you some time if you review the HUD Settlement Statement included within the loan docs to see at the end of the list if any money is due from the borrower to the title company. If so, remind the borrower that you will need a check in the amount requested.

Printing the Docs

Open the e-mail containing the attached docs. There will usually be two or three separate attachments. Open them in order and keep track of what you open so you don't duplicate. If you have a two-tray printer you merely print out the docs and let them fall where they may. If you have only a one-tray printer, hopefully, the title company has sent the legal and the letter size in separate attachments and has labeled them as such. Otherwise, you might have to guesstimate which is which.

If I am not sure about the size, I will print out one copy in legal size and one copy in letter size and then sort the documents into two separate piles. The first pile has the documents on the sizes of paper that matches the actual size of each page. The becomes the pile of documents that I go through with the borrowers and have them sign. The second pile of documents becomes the pile that I leave with the borrowers. Often the HUD docs are the legal size and the rest are mixed sizes. You will soon get the hang of it and develop your own system for separating the docs.

Remember that the Deed of Trust or Mortgage usually must be letter size. Check with your county's recorder to ascertain their preference for recording. In my county the recorder charges the title company a penalty fee if these docs are not in letter size.

There is no problem in determining the appropriate size when the docs are sent by overnight courier, either to you or to the borrower, because the package will contain two copies in the sizes required by the title company.

In those cases in which the docs are to be sent to the borrower, you would be wise to check with the borrower before leaving for the signing just to be sure that he or she has the docs. You also could advise the borrower during your initial contact to call you when the docs arrive.

Preparing the Docs for Signing

Place the borrower's copy in a folder or envelope so that you don't mix it with the copy to be signed. Review each page of the documents and do the following:

> ➢ As you read through the docs, list on your Notary Assignment Summary (described in Chapter 1) the documents that require notarization. You will then have the list ready to copy into your notary journal and you will know the number of notarizations you did to record on your Signing Log spread sheet.

> ➢ Note the wording of the acknowledgments or *jurats* included with the documents to be sure that it conforms to that required in you state. Prepare copies of your own acknowledgments and/or *jurats* if the wording does not conform.

➢ Buy a supply of small posties at your local office supply store and post each place that requires a signature, or an initial, or completion by the borrower. This will save time at the signing and will make the process less confusing for the borrower. It will also force you to note each that does require a signature or initials or completion that you might otherwise miss.

➢ Prepare one or two extra copies of your own acknowledgment and jurat, with the borrower's name typed in, just in case you need it. If the docs do not contain a Signature Affidavit, I add one of my own. The title company might need it, and I also count it as a document notarized, which, in my state, means $10.00 less that I have to report to Social Security as self-employment income from the amount I am paid for the signing.

➢ Contrary to what I and you might have been told about preparing documents for notarization, It is my practice to complete the notarization process (short of adding my signature) of each acknowledgment or *jurat* before going to the signing. That way I am sure that my seal is stamped clearly so as to be photographical. County recorders don't like blurred seals. This practice also saves me time at the actual signing, and avoids having to interrupt the borrower's signing with my notary work. After they have signed, I sign, and we move on.

➢ You will be given a return address for the signed docs, with the title company's account number, either in the instructions form the signing company or from the title company. Prepare a courier form (Fed Ex, UPS, HDL, OnTrack, etc.) and place it on the courier company's envelope, matching the size of the docs to return. If documents are sent to you or to the borrower, a return envelope is usually included. I should have mentioned earlier to obtain a supply of envelopes and label forms to have on hand.

➢ Know ahead of time the nearest location to the signing of the courier company's drop box. These are easily obtainable on-line from the company's web site.

The Signing

Arrive at the signing location a few minutes early, never late. If there is some unforeseen circumstances that prevents you from arriving on time, call the borrower and the signing company to let them know.

Dress in a professional manner, although it may be casual, but be neat and clean. Don't wear sandals, tennis shoes, shorts, or jeans and a tee shirt.

Identify yourself, but if you give out a business card, be sure that the borrower does not think you are soliciting business. I find the photo ID badge given me by the U. S. Mobile Notary Association very useful for this purpose. It clips on my shirt or coat pocket and looks professional.

Remember that this is YOUR signing. Don't be a control freak, but be in charge so as to expedite the signing in an organized manner to completion. Suggest a table or similar location where there will be sufficient room for you and all the signers to gather. Avoid having any food or drink at the table. If the borrower wants coffee or a soda, ask him or her to place it far away from the docs. If you make them worried enough, they won't have anything around that might spill.

Place the stack of documents in front of you, and hand them one at a time to the borrower to sign, initial, or complete. Your own *Assignment Disclosure and Hold Harmless Agreement* form should be the first document to have signed. Place it then in a location separate from the rest of the documents so that you will find it later for your file and it will not be shipped off with the rest of the documents.

Don't let the borrower have the documents to review first. He or she can do that as you go along with the signing. Remind him or her that you have a copy of the docs to leave with him or her. Record the identity

Document/s in you notary journal first, before proceeding with the signing, and be certain that it is current.

You can say what each document contains, but be certain **not to give advice or make judgmental comments**. Take each page signed or initialed by the borrower, review it for completion, and place it in a new stack. Be careful not to skip a page or to mix the signed with the unsigned.

Borrowers occasionally raise an issue over the closing costs shown on the HUD Settlement Statement or on the difference between the estimated closing costs and the final statement, the interest stated in the Truth-in-Lending Statement. Tell the borrower that you are not able to explain any such issues or questions and have him or her phone the loan broker right then. If their loan broker is unavailable, have them call the title company representative. If the loan is a re-fi line of credit, or reverse mortgage, explain that they have the three days to rescind the loan and that you will soon show them those documents. **If the borrower refused to continue with the signing**, call the signing company then and there, and let them decide how to proceed. If you leave a signing when the borrower refuses to continue, be sure to take both copies of the documents with you. The borrower is not entitled to a copy of the documents he or she did not sign.

After the signing has been completed, explain to the borrower that you need a few more minutes to review the documents just to be sure that nothing was missed. Then carefully **review each page** for signatures, initials, completion, and notarization requirements. Read each word of your acknowledgments to be sure that you have crossed out the pronouns and/or plurals not used. Did you sign correctly? Is your stamp correcctly placed?

Thank the borrower for his or her time and cooperation. Give them their copy of the docs and leave. Drive to some convenient location, perhaps to the courier drop site, and review the documents again. Review the signing process in your mind's eye: What did you forget to do or have the borrower do? Drop off the documents with the courier when you are sure that everything is correct.

Immediately, or as soon as is practical, phone the signing company to report the completed signing. Be prepared to give them the signing order number, borrower's name, name of the courier company, and tracking number. When you return home, you might also enter this information into the signing company's web site notary area.

Now you have several pages for the file on this signing: your Assignment Summary, the signing company's instructions, the Hold Harmless Agreement, and a copy of the courier shipping bill, unless you were give a pre-addressed self-ship label from the title company. Keep these together, and staple them, along with a printed   copy of the tracking notice once the documents have been delivered.   Complete your signing log, and note somewhere it and/or when you should invoice the signing company.

Keep track of the invoicing and when you are paid and for what signings you are paid. I was recently paid for June signings and was paid earlier for May signings, but I didn't show any payment from the company for April signings. I re-invoice them with a note that I had no record of be paid for April. I soon received a check for several hundred dollars for April the signings; an accounting oversight, I'm sure. Now get prepared for the next signing, and the next...

Chapter 6: Special Document Signing Procedures

Unique Notary Opportunities

There are five additional opportunities for notary signing agents to expand their area of expertise and increase their income. Two such opportunities are available exclusively through the National Notary Association under the title Trusted Enrollment Agent. NNA also offers a nationwide certified training program called eNotarization. The fourth opportunity is called eSign, a training program offered by AmTrust Mortgage Bank. A fifth opportunity is notarizing automotive loans documents.

Some of these opportunities are in their formative stage and you will need additional information from more direct sources, such as NNA, as these special document signing procedures mature. Nevertheless, this chapter introduces you to each of these opportunities.

The Trusted Enrollment Agent

According to the introduction offered by NNA:

The Trusted Enrollment Agent™ Program is the largest and most lucrative opportunity for Notaries since the Notary Signing Agent field opened up. It offers a whole new line of business for Notaries nationwide with excellent prospects for long-term career growth.

Trusted Enrollment Agents™ are paid to travel to offices to identify persons seeking electronic identity credentials. These credentials are now needed by professionals to send, receive and handle sensitive electronic documents. With identity-proofing being a significant component of a Trusted Enrollment Agent's™ role, Notaries already have many of the skills required to get started.

Trusted Enrollment Agents™ will earn:

- $35.00 per single enrollment — as little as a 15-minute appointment

- $85.00 for three enrollments at same location/time

- And more for additional signings

  Major aerospace, pharmaceutical and medical research organizations already insist on using only NNA Trusted Enrollment Agents™ — TEAs who have participated in a background screening and who have additional training.With electronic identity-proofing expanding into more business areas, a growing number of organizations will demand the services of NNA Trusted Enrollment Agents™.

The TEA program is operated by NNA in cooperation with Execostar, a company that offers a:

> Trusted Workspace powers secure, multi-enterprise information sharing, collaboration, and business process integration throughout the extended value chain. Exostar was founded in 2000 to support the complex trading needs of the world's largest aerospace and defense companies, including BAE SYSTEMS, The Boeing Company, Lockheed Martin Corp., Raytheon Co., and Rolls-Royce. Exostar's identity assurance products and on-demand business applications reduce risk, improve agility, and strengthen trading partner relationships and profitability for over 40,000 companies worldwide. For more information, please visit www.exostar.com.

Execostar gets requests from companies within the aerospace and defense industry to "clear" individuals for trusted employment. These requests are referred to NNA, who in turn refers the individual applications to a NNA certified notary who verifies the identification and clearance of the potential employee. Notaries must complete the Execostar certification training and exam process through NNA to qualify for these referrals.

TEA referrals to NNA also come from a company called SAIC, the Science Applications International Corporation. SAIC has approximately 44,000 employees and serves customers in the Department of Defense, the intelligence community, the U.S. Department of Homeland Security, other U.S. Government civil agencies and selected commercial markets.

A notary must also qualify through NNA to receive employee verification assignments from SAIC. Unfortunately for some notaries, TEA opportunities are available primarily in urban areas having a concentration of aerospace, defense, and related government agencies.

eNotarization

The use of an electronic notary seal (ENS) is a relatively new procedure accepted in some states by which a trained and certified notary uses an electronic notary seal stored in his or her computer to notarize documents that are accessed on-line or by the traditional paper notarization. According to NNA:

> Electronic documents offer speed, flexibility, economy and easy storage. The Electronic Notary Seal (ENS™) provides this necessary and final link for electronic notarizations.

The ENS™ is a unique digital certificate that confirms a Notary's commission. It is accessible only to its designated Notary. That Notary can protect the ENS by password or through a biometric (e.g., fingerprint) confirmation.

The ENS™ helps thwart forgeries and frauds. Once affixed, the ENS renders the document tamper-evident by marking in real time the moment when the Notary authenticated it. If someone later attempts to alter the e-document, subsequent viewers of the document can be alerted that tampering has occurred.

Like e-mail messages, word processing documents, Web pages and PDF files like Adobe Acrobat, the ENS™ is readable. Additionally, an image of the Notary's seal stamp can be included in any image file form to accompany it.

eSign Notarization

This might be termed a partial electronic notarization process, the use of paperless mortgage technology, in which a majority of the documents in a loan package are created and signed on-line (eSign) by the borrow. The primary provider of eSign is AmTrust

Mortgage Bank and is available from Gemstone (http://www.esignmortgage.com/about.html).

At a signing, the notary uses either his or her laptop of the borrower's computer, and a passcode, to access the eDocs through the Gemstone website. With a simple click of the mouse, the borrower consents to the eSign process, then click-signs a majority of the loan documents. The borrower or notary can save a copy of the documents to a CD rather than having to print out a set of paper docs for the borrower.

This process avoids the chance of missing a document in the signing and the cost and effort of shipping and storing paper. However, there still exists the need to paper sign and notarize a few documents, such as the Deed of Trust or mortgage.

The documents can be sent to the borrower ahead of time for his or her review in preparation for the signing. According to AmTrust:

> eSign is available for most table-funded Conforming Fixed, Conforming Portfolio Fixed, Conforming Standard ARM and Portfolio ARM programs. Interest-only and low documentation are additional eSign options. eSign utilizes all industry approved standards and requirements of authenticity

A number of title companies participate with AmTrust Mortgage using e-Sign, and they are listed on the web site: **http://www.esignmortgage.com**. That site also has a training and informational video you can watch for additional information. You can also access that site to complete their on-line training.

Automotive Document Signing

There is an emerging market for automotive document signing, especially in large urban areas, where individuals are buying new and used cars on-line. To date, the primary national company is Maverick Signing (**www.mavericksigning.com**).

Maverick acts as a liaison between the dealership and the clients, and refers the actual signing to certified notaries working within the client's area. Maverick will arrange the signing appointment time and place with the car dealer's customer, and confirm that arrangement with the dealer's finance manager, who is the primary contact person in facilitating the signing.

Documents are sent overnight to the notary, and will include a combination of state DMV forms, a sales or lease contract, a vehicle condition report, and possibly the title and keys to the car, along with other dealer specific documents. The notary will verify the identity of the car buyer, obtain a copy of his or her driver's license, and complete the signing as directed by the dealer. The notary might also accept certified funds from the car buyer to return to the dealer with the documents.

These automotive signings will usually be completed during hours when the dealership is open, or at least when the finance manager is available. The notary can communicate with the finance manager at any time during the signing if questions arise, and will report the completion of the signing to the finance manager, as well as to Maverick.

If you are a notary interested in doing automotive signings, you may sign up with Maverick and complete their on-line training. They provide a comprehensive training manual that you can use as an on-going reference for signings.

Summary

The availability and use of these special notary opportunities will vary with the location in which you work. Obviously, TEA opportunities will be more plentiful in the large urban sectors where defense, biomedical, and other research companies are located. The use of eSign and eNotarization will grow to keep pace with advancing technology. Much of this growth will depend on how well county recorders and the mortgage industry cooperate to develop compatible electronic technology that is fraud proof and affordable.

Chapter 7: Summing Up

Now you are ready. Be sure you are organized and prepared before you invite business. If you are, then luck will be yours. My definition of luck, however, is when preparation meets opportunity.

You have all the ingredients of your business established: a name that is short and memorable, business cards, a DBA on file, a web site, an assignment summary sheet, a signing log spread sheet on your computer, and your hold-harmless ready for singing.

Sign up with as many of the high rated signing companies as you dare, and be prepared to take a quiz or two with some of them. When you sign up, they will ask for your hours of availability. Be specific and complete. When I was going to college some years ago, I took an on-call job at a local juvenile hall to earn money while working around my college schedule. A friend of mine worked there too, and he gave me some advice to consider if I wanted to be called for work: after you give them your available hours, "always be home, always answer the phone, and always say *yes.*"

I offer that same advice to you if you want signing companies to call you again, and again, and again. They want someone they can count on and who does credible work. Once called, always follow their instructions to the letter, and keep them informed of the signing progress.

Be prompt in arriving at the signing location. Dress appropriately. Make professionalism the hallmark of your signing process. Don't be a control freak, but remember that it is your signing, so be in charge and control the signing process to a positive completion. Be creative and enjoy the efforts.

Selected Forms for Review

Signature Affidavit

This is my true and correct legal signature and it does in fact say _____ (Name must match loan documents).

This is to certify that my legal signature is as written below. This signature must exactly match signatures on the Note and Deed of Trust.

I hereby understand that my lender may reject my signature if they feel that it appears to be undersigned. My lender could charge additional fees if they need to redraw the loan documents.

I am also known as, or have credit under the following names

_____   _____

Print name   **Signature**

Jurat

State of _____
County of Lilliput

Subscribed and sworn to (or affirmed) before me on this 4th day of July, 2076, by John Quincy Public, who proved to me on the basis of satisfactory evidence to be the person(s) who appeared before me

Signature_____   (Seal)
James J. Meeker

Corrections Agreement / Limited Power of Attorney

The undersigned borrower(s) for and in consideration of the approval, closing, and funding of their mortgage loan, hereby grant _____(Lender)_____ its successors, and/or assigns as lender, limited power of attorney to correct and/or execute or initial all typographical or clerical errors discovered in any or all of the closing documentation required to be executed by the undersigned at settlement. In the event this limited power of attorney is exercised, the undersigned will be notified and receive a copy of the document(s) executed or initialed on his/their behalf.

THIS LIMITED POWER OF ATTORNEY MAY NOT BE USED TO INCREASE THE INTEREST RATE THE UNDERSIGNED IS PAYING, INCREASETHE TERM OF THE UNDERSSIGNED'S LOAN, INCREASE THE UNDERSIGNED'S OUTSTANDING PRINCIPAL BALANCE, OR INCREASE THE UNDERSIGNED'S MONTHLY PRINCIPAL AND INTEREST PAYMENTS. Any of these specified changes must be executed directly by the undersigned.

This limited power of attorney shall automatically terminate 180 days from the closing date of the undersigned's mortgage loan.

IN WITNESS WHEREOF, the undersigned has/have executed this Limited Power of Attorney as of the date referenced below.

Signature_____
Printed Name _____

(Your State's acknowledgment or Jurat)

Signature and seal

CERTIFICATION OF TRUST

(Pursuant to California Probate Code §18100.5)

I/We,

_____,

trustee(s) confirm the following facts:

1. The

_____(Name of

Trust) is currently in existence and was executed on

_____

2. The settler(s) of the trust are:

_____

3. The currently acting trustee(s) of the trust is (are):

_____

4. The power of the trustee(s) includes:

     a. The powers to sell, convey and exchange YES NO (*please check one*)

     b. The power to borrow money and encumber the trust property with a deed of trust or mortgage

YES NO (*please check one*)

5. The trust _____REVOCABLE _____ IRREVOCABLE (*please check one*) and the following party(ies), if any, is (are) identified as having the power to revoke the trust:

_____

6. The trust _____DOES _____DOES NOT (*please check one*) have multiple trustees. If the trust has multiple trustees, the signatures of: *please mark one of the following*

_____ALL

_____ANY (*specify number*) of the Trustees are required to exercise the powers of the Trust.

7. The Trust identification number is: _____
      (*Social Security No. /Employer ID*).

8. Title to trust assets is to be taken in the following manner:

_____

_____

The undersigned trustee(s) declare(s) that the trust has not been revoked, modified or amended in any manner which would cause the representations contained herein to be incorrect. This Certification is executed by all of the currently acting trustees of the Trust pursuant to Section 18100.5 of the Probate Code.

_____   _____

James Quincy Public   Jane Eyer Public

(Your State's acknowledgment or Jurat)

Signature and seal

GRANT DEED

RECORDING REQUESTED BY:

True Trust Mortgage, Inc.

When recorded, Mail documents

To:

John Q. Public
523 Oak Street
Lilliput, CA 9999
APN: 123-321-213

The undersigned grantor(s) John Quincy. Public, a married man who acquired title as John Quincy Public, an unmarried man:

Documentary transfer tax is $0.00   City transfer tax is $0.00

( )   computed on full value of property conveyed, or

( )   computed on full value less value of liens or encumbrances remaining at time of sale

( )   unincorporated area: City of Lilliput

FOR NO CONSIDERATION, receipt of which is hereby acknowledged, John Q. Public, a married man who acquired title as John Quincy Public, an unmarried man

Hereby GRANT(S) to John Quincy Public and Jane Zero Public, husband and wife as joint tenants with rights of survivorship

The following described property in the City of Lilliput, County of Sonoma, State of California. SEE EXHIBIT "A" ATTACHED HERETP AND MADE A PART HEREOF

Dated:_____   Signature
_____

(Your state's acknowledgment, signature and seal)

DEED OF TRUST

Recording requested by;

Return to:

True Faith Financial

191715 Financial Road, Lilliput, CA

Loan NO: 1776

MIN 1001818 -9

MERS TELEPHONE: (999) 595-9999

DEFINITIONS

Words used in multiple sections of this document are defined below and other words are defined in Sections 3, 11, 14, 18, 20, and 26. Certain rules regarding the usage of words used in this document are provided in Section 10.

(A) **"Security Instrument"** means this document, which is dated July 4, 2076, together with all Riders in this document

(B) **"BORROWERS"** are John Quincy Public and Jane Eyre Public, as **JOINT TENANTS.** Borrowers' address is 1721 Adams Drive, Lilliput, California, 95555. Borrowers are the trustors under this Security Agreement.

(C)**"LENDER"** IS True Faith Financial, Inc. Lender is a corporation organized and existing under the laws of the State of California. Lender's address is: 191715 Financial Road, Lilliput, California.

(D) **"Trustee is** Third Nevada Title and Escrow company, Inc, a Nevada corporation

(E) **"MERS"** is Mortgage Electronic Registration Systems, Inc. MERS is a separate corporation that is acting solely as a nominee for the Lender and Lender's successors and assign. MERS is the beneficiary under this Security Instrument. MERS is organized and existing under the laws of Delaware, and has an address and telephone number of.............................

(F) 'NOTE" means the promissory note sinned by Borrowers and dated July 4, 2076. The note states that Borrowers owe Lender **Seven Hundred forty Thousand and 00/100 dollars (U.S. $740,000.00,** plus interest. Borrowers have promised to pay this debt in regular payments and to pay the debt in full not later than June 31, 3006.

Your state's acknowledgment, signature and seal)

This Deed of Trust continues on for some twelve to fourteen pages that detail the full essence of the security agreement. The borrower initials each page at the bottom, with some lenders, and not with other lenders. The borrower signs the final page, by which he or she agrees to abide by the terms of the agreement and the accompanying Note, and pledges the property as security for the loan. You, the notary, complete either the accompanying acknowledgment or include your own acknowledgment, depending upon the required wording.

Notary Assignment Summary

Borrower/s: _____

Address:_____

Lender:_____   Title Company: _____

Loan Number : _____   File No: _____

Phone: _____

Appointment Location:
Signing Co:

Appointment Arrangements:
_____

Appointment arranged by: _____
Contact & Phone:

Documents possessed by: _____

Document Package Returned:
      Sent to: _____

      Address: _____

      City, State: _____

      Co Acct # _____   **PH:** _____

      Company Used to Send: _____

      Tracking No:

_____

      Drop Location: _____

Mileage & Expenses
Total miles: __
Sign Fee:_____

Documents NOTARIZED:
_____
_____
_____
_____
--
_____
_____
_____
_____

Assignment Disclosure & Hold Harmless Agreement

Borrower(s): _____

Address:_____

Lender:_____   Title Company: _____

Loan Number : _____   File No: _____

This form is to explain my role and responsibilities, in the signing of your loan documents.

1.   In signing this document, the undersigned(s) understands and acknowledges that I, _____ Notary Public, am an independent contractor, functioning as a mobile notary. The lender, broker, title company, or signing service does not employ me as a regular employee. I am limited to explaining the general purpose of the documents enclosed and am prohibited from providing any detailed explanations; please contact your broker or loan officer with these questions and/or concerns. I am not an attorney or an accountant and I can not give legal or financial advice. I am, however, screened and approved by the State Department of Justice, the FBI, and the National Notary Association to handle confidential documents, and I am commissioned by the California Secretary of State to serve as a notary.

2.   I make no guarantees or implied warranties as to the character, content, or accuracy of the information contained within the loan documents, nor do I take any responsibility for the timely closing of your loan transaction.

3.   By signing this document, the borrower(s) also:

- Solemnly swear or affirm, under penalties of perjury, that all statements you will make or sign for will be truthful and correct, to the best of your knowledge and belief.

- Have full knowledge of the transaction and understand the possible implications of and consequences of signing the documents.

- Are entering into this transaction and signing of your own free will, and you intend to abide by the commitments made therein.

- Agrees to hold me harmless from any errors, omissions, or negligence that is beyond the scope of my legal and professional responsibilities as a notary public.

4.   Please sign all documents *as your name appears*, including middle initial or name, on each document where indicated.   Initial, sign and date for yourself. Borrower(s) may not date for each other.

_____   Date:_____

Borrower

NOTES

Made in the USA
Monee, IL
03 February 2021

59518470R00046